WHEN THE WIND BLOWS

GENERAL EDITOR

JACK BOOTH

❧

DAVID BOOTH

WILLA PAULI & JO PHENIX

IMPRESSIONS

HOLT, RINEHART AND WINSTON OF CANADA, LIMITED

Sponsoring Editor: Sheba Meland
Senior Editor: Wendy Cochran
Production Editor: Jocelyn Van Huyse
Art Director: Wycliffe Smith
Design Assistant: Julia Naimska
Cover Illustrator: Heather Cooper

ISBN 0-03-921404-4

Canadian Cataloguing in Publication Data

Main entry under title:
When the Wind Blows

(Impressions)
For use in schools.
ISBN 0-03-921404-4

1. Readers (Primary).   2. Readers – 1950 –
I. Booth, Jack   II. Series.

PE1119.C34   428.6   C83-098247-7

Illustrations
Arnold Lobel: pp. 4-6; *Philippe Béha*: pp. 7, 28, 87-98; *Jean-Christian Knaff*: pp. 8-13, 46-53; *Richard Hefter*: pp. 14-17; *Eugenie Fernandés*: pp. 18-19; *Leslie Fairfield*: pp. 20-28; *Ken Stampnick*: pp. 29-38; *Ilze Bertuss*: pp. 39-45; *Robert Kraus*: pp. 54-62; *John Burningham*: pp. 63-66; *Stan Mack*: pp. 67-77; *Clive Dobson*: pp. 78-79; *Terry Nell Morris*: pp. 80-84; *Joe Weissmann*: pp. 85-86; *Vladyana Krykorka*: pp. 99-101, 111-112; *Barbara Klunder*: pp. 102-109; *Wendy Cochran*: p. 110.

The authors and publishers gratefully acknowledge the consultants listed below for their contribution to the development of this program:

Isobel Bryan   *Primary Consultant   Ottawa Board of Education*
Ethel Buchanan   *Language Arts Consultant   Winnipeg, Manitoba*
Heather Hayes   *Elementary Curriculum Consultant   City of Halifax Board of Education*
Gary Heck   *Curriculum Co-ordinator, Humanities   Lethbridge School District No. 51*
Ina Mary Rutherford   *Supervisor of Reading and Primary Instruction   Bruce County Board of Education*
Janice M. Sarkissian   *Supervisor of Instruction (Primary and Pre-School)   Greater Victoria School District*
Lynn Taylor   *Language Arts Consultant   Saskatoon Catholic School Board*

Acknowledgements
Nursery Rhyme Friends: "Jerry Hall," with illustration, "One Day a Boy Went Walking," with illustration, "Handy-Spandy," with illustration, from GREGORY GRIGGS AND OTHER NURSERY RHYME PEOPLE. Selected and illustrated by Arnold Lobel. Copyright © 1978 by Arnold Lobel. By permission of Greenwillow Books (A Division of William Morrow & Company). *Pairs of Bears*: Excerpt from NOSES AND TOES, an up and down and in and out book by Richard Hefter. Copyright © 1974 by One Strawberry, Inc. TM. *The Little Turtle*: Copyright © by Macmillan Publishing Co., Inc., renewed 1948 by Elizabeth C. Lindsay. Reprinted with permission of Macmillan Publishing Co., Inc. From COLLECTED POEMS by Vachel Lindsay. *I Love Every People*: From I LOVE EVERY PEOPLE BY Florence Parry Heide. Copyright © 1978 Concordia Publishing House. Used by permission. *My Son the Mouse*: Selected text and art from MY SON THE MOUSE by Robert Kraus. Reprinted by permission of the author, Robert Kraus. *The Snow*: Written and illustrated by John Burningham (Thomas Y. Crowell Co.) Copyright © 1974 by John Burningham. By permission of Jonathan Cape Ltd. and Harper & Row, Publishers, Inc. EMILY & ARTHUR by Domitille de Pressense English translation © 1977 Ebbitt Cutler of the original French EMILIE et ARTHUR © 1975 Editions G.P., Paris reprinted by permission of the Canadian Publisher Tundra Books. *Ten Bears in My Bed*: From TEN BEARS IN MY BED: A GOODNIGHT COUNTDOWN by Stan Mack. Copyright © 1974 by Stan Mack. Reprinted by permission of Pantheon Books, a Division of Random House, Inc. *Lucky Puppy, Lucky Boy*: From LUCKY PUPPY! LUCKY BOY!, by Terry Nell Morris. Copyright © 1980 by Random House, Inc. Reprinted by permission of Alfred A. Knopf, Inc. *The Chick and the Duckling*: Copyright © 1972 by Mirra Ginsburg. Reprinted with permission of Macmillan Publishing Co., Inc. From THE CHICK AND THE DUCKLING by Mirra Ginsburg.

Care has been taken to trace the ownership of copyright material used in this text. The publishers will welcome any information enabling them to rectify any reference or credit in subsequent editions.

Printed in Canada   7 8 9   91 90 89 88

Table of Contents

Nursery Rhyme Friends
Traditional

Jerry Hall
He is so small,
A rat could eat him,
Hat and all.

One day a boy went walking
And walked into a store.
He bought a pound of sausage meat,
And laid it on the floor.
The boy began to whistle—
He whistled up a tune,
And all the little sausages
Danced around the room.

Handy-spandy,
Jack-a-Dandy,
Loves plum cake
and sugar candy.
He bought some
at a grocer's shop,
And out he came,
hop, hop, hop, hop.

In a Dark, Dark Wood
Traditional

In a dark, dark wood

there was a dark, dark house.

And in that dark, dark house

there was a dark, dark room.

And in that dark, dark room

there was a dark, dark cupboard.

And in that dark, dark cupboard

there was a dark, dark shelf.

And on that dark, dark shelf

there was a dark, dark box.

And in that dark, dark box there was...

Six Little Ducks
Traditional

Six little ducks
went swimming one day
Over the pond and far away.

Mother duck said,
"Quack, quack, quack."
And five little ducks
went swimming right back.

Five little ducks
went swimming one day
Over the pond and far away.

Mother duck said,
"Quack, quack, quack."
And four little ducks
went swimming right back.

Four little ducks
went swimming one day
Over the pond and far away.

Mother duck said,
"Quack, quack, quack."

And three little ducks
went swimming right back.

Three little ducks
went swimming one day
Over the pond and far away.

Mother duck said,
"Quack, quack, quack."

And two little ducks
went swimming right back.

Two little ducks
went swimming one day
Over the pond and far away.

Mother duck said,
"Quack, quack, quack."
And one little duck
went swimming right back.

One little duck
went swimming one day
Over the pond and far away.

Mother duck said,
"Quack, quack, quack."
And no little ducks
went swimming right back.

Pairs of Bears

by
Richard Hefter

Pears on bears

Bears in chairs

Pairs of bears with chairs
going up the stairs

Hairy pairs of bears
running down the stairs

and out the door

Going to School
by
Meguido Zola

Mom and the dog walked Madeline to school.
They walked out of the apartment,

down three floors,
out the front door,

into the street,
up two blocks,

into the playground,
across the school yard,

between the red buildings,
up the stairs,

through the two doors,
past the principal's office,

behind the big gym,
down into the basement,

through the green door,
and into the classroom.

The Little Turtle
by
Vachel Lindsay

There was   a little turtle.
He lived   in a box.
He swam   in a puddle.
He climbed   on the rocks.

He snapped at a mosquito.
He snapped at a flea.
He snapped at a minnow.
And he snapped at me.

He caught the mosquito.
He caught the flea.
He caught the minnow.
But he didn't catch me!

The Empty House

by

David Booth

When I got home from school
I went into the house.
No one was there.

I went into the hall.
No one was there.

I went into the kitchen.
No one was there.

I went into the living room.
No one was there.

I went into the family room.
No one was there.

I went into the bedroom.
No one was there.

I went into the bathroom.
No one was there.

I went into the basement.
No one was there.

I went into the back yard.

Everyone was there!
They all sang
HAPPY BIRTHDAY to me.

A Is an Apple Pie

Adapted by Willa Pauli

A is an apple pie.

C cuts it.

B bakes it.

D drops it.

E eats it.

F fights for it.

G gets it.

H has it.

I inspects it.

J jumps for it.

K keeps it.

L loves it.

M munches it.

N needs it.

O orders it.

P pecks at it.

Q quarters it.

R refuses it.

S steals it.

T takes it.

U upsets it.

V views it.

W wants it.

X Y Z
eat the pie in bed.

I Love Every People
by
Florence Parry Heide

work people

play people

night people

day people

old people

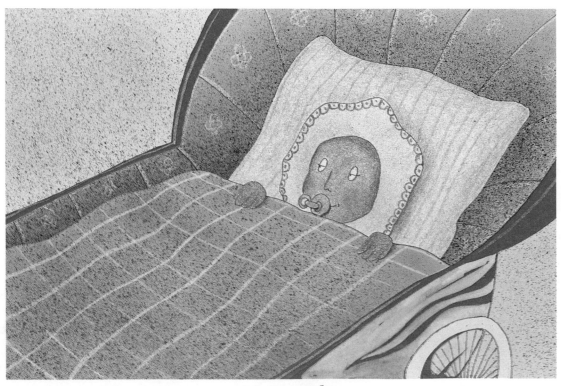

new people

sit people

do people

fast people

slow people

stay people

go people

I love every people!

My Son the Mouse

by
Robert Kraus

LIKE A LION.

IS HE GENTLE?

LIKE A LAMB.

DOES HE EAT?

LIKE A HORSE.

DOES HE SLEEP?

LIKE A LOG.

CAN HE SING?

LIKE A

BIRD.

CAN HE
DANCE?

LIKE A BEAR.

WHAT WILL HE BE WHEN HE GROWS UP?

A DOCTOR, OF COURSE.

ARE YOU PROUD?

LIKE A PEACOCK.

The Snow
by
John Burningham

One day it snowed.

Mommy and I rolled
a big snowball.

We made a snowman.

Mommy pulled me.

But I fell off.

I lost my glove
and I was cold.

So we went indoors.

I hope the snow
is here tomorrow.

Ten Bears in My Bed

by
Stan Mack

There were **10** in his bed
and the little one said

Roll over!
Roll over!

So they all rolled over
and one **flew** out.

There were **9** in his bed
and the little one said

Roll over!
Roll over!

So they all rolled over
and one **galloped** out.

There were **8** in his bed
and the little one said

Roll over!
Roll over!

So they all rolled over
and one **skated** out.

There were **7** in his bed
and the little one said

Roll over!
Roll over!

So they all rolled over
and one **roared** out.

There were **6** in his bed
and the little one said

Roll over!
Roll over!

So they all rolled over
and one **chugged** out.

There were **5** in his bed
and the little one said

Roll over!
Roll over!

So they all rolled over
and one **jumped** out.

There were **4** in his bed
and the little one said

Roll over!
Roll over!

So they all rolled over
and one **bounced** out.

There were **3** in his bed
and the little one said

Roll over!
Roll over!

So they all rolled over
and one **pedaled** out.

There were **2** in his bed
and the little one said

Roll over!
Roll over!

So they all rolled over
and one **tootled** out.

There was **1** in his bed
and the little one said

Roll over!
Roll over!

So one rolled over
and he **rumbled** out.

There were **none** in his bed
so the little one said...

Good night.

Lucky Puppy, Lucky Boy
by
Terry Nell Morris

Five Little Monkeys
Traditional

Five little monkeys jumping on the bed,
   One fell off and bumped his head.
Mama called the doctor, the doctor said:
"No more monkeys jumping on the bed!"

Four little monkeys jumping on the bed,
   One fell off and bumped her head.
Mama called the doctor, the doctor said:
"No more monkeys jumping on the bed!"

Three little monkeys jumping on the bed,
   One fell off and bumped his head.
Mama called the doctor, the doctor said:
"No more monkeys jumping on the bed!"

Two little monkeys jumping on the bed,
   One fell off and bumped her head.
Mama called the doctor, the doctor said:
"No more monkeys jumping on the bed!"

One little monkey jumping on the bed,
   One fell off and bumped his head.
Mama called the doctor, the doctor said:
"No more monkeys jumping on the bed!"

No little monkeys jumping on the bed,
   None fell off and bumped their heads.
Mama called the doctor, the doctor said:
"Put those monkeys right to bed!"

Emily and Arthur

by
Domitille de Préssensé

One morning Emily
could not find
Arthur.

Where was Arthur?
She loved
Arthur.

She looked
under
her bed,
and she found...

her pretty green
and white necklace.

She looked
behind
her chair,
and she found...

her teddy bear's
paw.

She opened
her closet,
and she found...

her little
storybook
and her long
stocking.

But not Arthur!

"Arthur, Arthur,
where are you?"

"Come on,"
said Stephen,
"maybe Arthur
is in the garden."

They looked
under the flowers...
and found
a family of snails.

They looked
near the well...
and found
a family of lizards.

They looked
among the lettuce...

and found
a family of hedgehogs.

And there was
Arthur.

Arthur
was with
his father,
his mother,
and all
his brothers
and sisters.

And Emily laughed.

She had
found
Arthur,

her green and
white necklace,

the paw of
her teddy bear,

her little
storybook,

and her
long stocking.

Emily was very happy.

Fire! Fire!
Traditional

"Fire! Fire!"
Cried Mrs. McGuire.

"Where? Where?"
Cried Mr. Blair.

"All over town!"
Cried Miss Brown.

"Get some water!"
Cried Ms. Potter.

"We'd better jump!"
Cried Mrs. Gump.

"That would be silly!"
Cried Mr. Brunilly.

"It looks too risky!"
Cried Ms. Matriski.

"What'll we do?"
Cried Mrs. La Rue.

"Turn in the alarm!"
Cried Mr. La Farme.

"Save us! Save us!"
Cried Miss Potayvus.

The Chick and the Duckling

by
Mirra Ginsburg

A Duckling came out
of the shell.

"I am out!"
he said.

"Me too,"
said the Chick.

"I am taking a walk,"
said the Duckling.

"Me too,"
said the Chick.

"I am digging a hole,"
said the Duckling.

"Me too,"
said the Chick.

"I found a worm,"
said the Duckling.

"Me too,"
said the Chick.

"I caught
a butterfly,"
said the Duckling.

"Me too,"
said the Chick.

"I am going
for a swim,"
said the Duckling.

"Me too,"
said the Chick.

"I am swimming,"
said the Duckling.

"Me too!"
cried the Chick.

The Duckling pulled
the Chick out.

"I'm going for another swim,"
said the Duckling.

"Not me,"
said the Chick.

My Bedtime Rules

by
David Booth

Every night
before I go to bed
I follow my bedtime rules:

1. Ask to watch one more television show.

2. Ask to hear a story read aloud.

3. Ask for a glass of orange juice.

4. Ask for the window open.

5. Dream wonderful dreams about not going to bed.

Goodnight
by
David Booth

"Goodnight, Mother."

"Goodnight, John."

"Goodnight, Father."

"Goodnight, John."

"Goodnight, Brother."

"Goodnight, John."

"Goodnight, Sister."

"Goodnight, John."

"Goodnight, Pale Moon."
"Go to sleep, John."

"Goodnight, Star."
"Go to sleep, John."

"Goodnight, Tree."
"Go to sleep, John!"

"Goodnight, Owl."
"Go to sleep, John!"

"SHHHHH—
John is asleep."

"Sleep softly, John."